# Sing-Along
# CHRISTMAS CAROLS

hinkler

*This book belongs to*

Ellie McMillan

Published by Hinkler Books Pty Ltd
45–55 Fairchild Street
Heatherton Victoria 3202 Australia
www.hinkler.com.au

# hinkler

Hinkler Books Pty Ltd 2012

Illustrations, design and layout © Hinkler Books Pty Ltd 2012
Sound Recording © Love to Sing Ltd, Linda Adamson 2012
Arrangements © Love to Sing Ltd, Linda Adamson 2012

www.childrenlovetosing.com

Cover Design: Hinkler Design Studio
Editor: Suzannah Pearce
Designers: Leanne Blanche, Melissa Chan, Ruth Comey, Anne Stanhope
Illustrations: Brijbasi Art Press Ltd, Graphics Manufacture, Melissa Webb
Prepress: Graphic Print Group

ISBN: 978 1 7430 8851 7

Printed and bound in China

# Contents

## Christmas Carols

Jingle Bells............................................8

Ding Dong Merrily on High.............. 10

Hark! The Herald Angels Sing........... 11

O Christmas Tree ............................. 12

Deck the Halls ................................. 13

Joy to the World ............................... 14

Twelve Days of Christmas ................. 16

A Christmas Lullaby........................... 20

We Three Kings................................. 21

Good King Wenceslas ...................... 22

Holly and the Ivy ............................. 24

O Holy Night!.................................. 26

God Rest You Merry, Gentlemen...... 28

O Little Town of Bethlehem ............. 30

Here We Come A-Carolling ............. 32

The Friendly Beasts ......................... 34

While Shepherds Watched Their
Flocks by Night..................................... 36

I Saw Three Ships ............................. 38

The Virgin Mary Had a Baby Boy .... 41

The First Noel.................................. 42

What Child is This? ........................... 44

Silent Night....................................... 45

Infant Holy, Infant Lowly ................. 46

Away in a Manger.............................. 47

We Wish You a Merry Christmas...... 48

## Christmas Stories

A Christmas Carol ............................. 50

The Night Before Christmas ............. 68

Santa's Helpers.................................. 72

Little Girl's Christmas........................ 74

The Gift of the Magi.......................... 88

# Christmas Carols

# Jingle Bells

*Words by James Lord Pierpont*

Dashing through the snow
In a one-horse open sleigh,
O'er the fields we go,
Laughing all the way.
Bells on bobtail ring,
Making spirits bright,
What fun it is to ride and sing
A sleighing song tonight, oh!

**Chorus:**

Jingle bells, jingle bells,
Jingle all the way;
Oh what fun it is to ride
In a one-horse open sleigh, hey!
Jingle bells, jingle bells,
Jingle all the way;
Oh what fun it is to ride
In a one-horse open sleigh.

Now the ground is white,
Go it while you're young,
Take the girls tonight,
Sing this sleighing song;
Get a bobtailed bay,
Two forty for his speed,
And hitch him to an open sleigh
And you will take the lead, oh!

Oh what fun it is to ride
In a one-horse open sleigh.

**Chorus**

# DING DONG MERRILY ON HIGH

*Words by George Woodward*

Ding dong! Merrily on high
In heav'n the bells are ringing,
Ding dong! Verily the sky
Is riv'n with angel singing.

**Chorus:**

Gloria,
Hosanna in excelsis!

E'en so here below, below,
Let steeple bells be swungen,
And 'Io, io, io!'
By priest and people sungen.

**Chorus**

Pray you, dutifully prime
Your matin chime, ye ringers;
May you beautifully rime
Your evetime song, ye singers.

**Chorus**

# Hark! The Herald Angels Sing

*Words by Charles Wesley*

Hark! The herald angels sing,
'Glory to the newborn King!
Peace on earth, and mercy mild,
God and sinners reconciled!'
Joyful, all ye nations rise,
Join the triumph of the skies;
With th' angelic host proclaim,
'Christ is born in Bethlehem!'

**Chorus:**

Hark! The herald angels sing,
'Glory to the newborn King!'

Christ, by highest heav'n adored;
Christ, the everlasting Lord!
Late in time behold Him come,
Offspring of a virgin's womb.
Veiled in flesh the Godhead see;
Hail th' incarnate Deity,
Pleased with us in flesh to dwell,
Jesus, our Emmanuel.

**Chorus**

Hail the heav'n-born Prince of Peace!
Hail the Son of Righteousness!
Light and life to all He brings,
Ris'n with healing in His wings.
Mild He lays His glory by,
Born that we no more may die,
Born to raise us from the earth,
Born to give us second birth.

**Chorus**

# O CHRISTMAS TREE

*Traditional German carol*

O Christmas tree! O Christmas tree!
You stand in splendid beauty;
O Christmas tree! O Christmas tree!
You stand in splendid beauty;
Your branches green in summer's glow,
And evergreen in winter's snow.
O Christmas tree! O Christmas tree!
You stand in splendid beauty.

O Christmas tree! O Christmas tree!
You stand in splendid beauty;
O Christmas tree! O Christmas tree!
You stand in splendid beauty;
Your branches green in summer's glow,
And evergreen in winter's snow.
O Christmas tree! O Christmas tree!
You stand in splendid beauty.

# Deck the Halls

*Traditional Welsh carol*

Deck the halls with boughs
of holly,
Fa la la la la, la la la la.
'Tis the season to be jolly,
Fa la la la la, la la la la.
Don we now our gay apparel,
Fa la la, la la la, la la la.
Troll the ancient yuletide carol,
Fa la la la la, la la la la.

See the blazing yule before us,
Fa la la la la, la la la la.
Strike the harp and join the chorus,
Fa la la la la, la la la la.
Follow me in merry measure,
Fa la la, la la la, la la la.
While I tell of yuletide treasure,
Fa la la la la, la la la la.

Fast away the old year passes,
Fa la la la la, la la la la.
Hail the new, ye lads and lasses,
Fa la la la la, la la la la.
Sing we joyous, all together,
Fa la la, la la la, la la la.
Heedless of the wind and weather,
Fa la la la la, la la la la.
Fa la la la la, la la la la.

14

# Joy to the World

*Words by Isaac Watts*

Joy to the world! The Lord is come!
Let earth receive her King;
Let every heart prepare Him room,
And heaven and nature sing,
And heaven and nature sing,
And heaven, and heaven, and nature sing.

Joy to the Earth! The Saviour reigns!
Let men their songs employ;
While fields and floods, rocks, hills, and plains
Repeat the sounding joy,
Repeat the sounding joy,
Repeat, repeat the sounding joy.

No more let sins and sorrows grow,
Nor thorns infest the ground;
He comes to make His blessings flow
Far as the curse is found,
Far as the curse is found,
Far as, far as, the curse is found.

He rules the world with truth and grace,
And makes the nations prove
The glories of His righteousness,
And wonders of His love,
And wonders of His love,
And wonders, wonders, of His love.

# Twelve Days of Christmas

*Traditional carol*

On the first day of Christmas,
My true love sent to me
A partridge in a pear tree.

On the second day of Christmas,
My true love sent to me
Two turtle doves,
And a partridge in a pear tree.

On the third day of Christmas,
My true love sent to me
Three French hens,
Two turtle doves,
And a partridge in a pear tree.

On the fourth day of Christmas,
My true love sent to me
Four calling birds,
Three French hens,
Two turtle doves,
And a partridge in a pear tree.

On the fifth day of Christmas,
My true love sent to me
Five golden rings,
Four calling birds,
Three French hens,
Two turtle doves,
And a partridge in a pear tree.

On the sixth day of Christmas,
My true love sent to me
Six geese a-laying,
Five golden rings,
Four calling birds,
Three French hens,
Two turtle doves,
And a partridge in a pear tree.

On the seventh day of Christmas,
My true love sent to me
Seven swans a-swimming,
Six geese a-laying,
Five golden rings,
Four calling birds,
Three French hens,
Two turtle doves,
And a partridge in a pear tree.

On the eighth day of Christmas,
My true love sent to me
Eight maids a-milking,
Seven swans a-swimming,
Six geese a-laying,
Five golden rings,
Four calling birds,
Three French hens,
Two turtle doves,
And a partridge in a pear tree.

On the ninth day of Christmas,
My true love sent to me
Nine ladies dancing,
Eight maids a-milking,
Seven swans a-swimming,
Six geese a-laying,
Five golden rings,
Four calling birds,
Three French hens,
Two turtle doves,
And a partridge in a pear tree.

On the tenth day of Christmas,
My true love sent to me
Ten lords a-leaping,
Nine ladies dancing,
Eight maids a-milking,
Seven swans a-swimming,
Six geese a-laying,
Five golden rings,
Four calling birds,
Three French hens,
Two turtle doves,
And a partridge in a pear tree.

On the eleventh day of Christmas,
My true love sent to me
Eleven pipers piping,
Ten lords a-leaping,
Nine ladies dancing,
Eight maids a-milking,
Seven swans a-swimming,
Six geese a-laying,
Five golden rings,
Four calling birds,
Three French hens,
Two turtle doves,
And a partridge in a pear tree.

On the twelfth day of Christmas,
My true love sent to me
Twelve drummers drumming,
Eleven pipers piping,
Ten lords a-leaping,
Nine ladies dancing,
Eight maids a-milking,
Seven swans a-swimming,
Six geese a-laying,
Five golden rings,
Four calling birds,
Three French hens,
Two turtle doves,
And a partridge in a pear tree!

# A Christmas Lullaby

*From Christmas Entertainments by Alice M. Kellogg, author unknown*
*Sing to the tune of the carol Silent Night*

Hushaby, hushaby,
Christmas stars are in the sky;
Sweet the bells of Christmas Eve —
Babies, each a kiss receive —
Hushaby, goodnight,
Hushaby, goodnight!

Lullaby, lullaby,
Babies in their cradles lie;
Every one in white is gowned,
Hush, make not a single sound!
Lullaby, goodnight,
Lullaby, goodnight!

Rockaby, rockaby,
Christmastide draweth nigh;
Quiet now the tiny feet,
Babies sleep so still and sweet —
Sweetest dreams, goodnight,
Sweetest dreams, goodnight!

# We Three Kings

*Words by John Henry Hopkins*

We three kings of Orient are,
Bearing gifts we traverse afar,
Field and fountain, moor and mountain,
Following yonder star.

**Chorus:**

O Star of wonder, star of night,
Star with royal beauty bright,
Westward leading, still proceeding,
Guide us to thy perfect light.

Born a King on Bethlehem's plain,
Gold I bring to crown Him again,
King forever, ceasing never,
Over us all to reign.

**Chorus**

Frankincense to offer have I,
Incense owns a Deity nigh,
Prayer and praising, voices raising,
Worship Him, God most high.

**Chorus**

Myrrh is mine, its bitter perfume,
Breathes a life of gathering gloom,
Sorrowing, sighing, bleeding, dying,
Sealed in the stone-cold tomb.

**Chorus**

Glorious now behold Him arise,
King and God and sacrifice,
Heaven sings, 'Alleluia!'
'Alleluia!' the Earth replies.

**Chorus**

# GOOD KING WENCESLAS

*Words by John Mason Neale*

Good King Wenceslas looked out,
On the feast of Stephen,
When the snow lay round about,
Deep and crisp and even.
Brightly shone the moon that night,
Though the frost was cruel,
When a poor man came in sight,
Gath'ring winter fuel.

'Hither, page, and stand by me,
If thou know'st it, telling,
Yonder peasant, who is he?
Where and what his dwelling?'
'Sire, he lives a good league hence,
Underneath the mountain,
Right against the forest fence,
By Saint Agnes' fountain.'

'Bring me food and bring me wine,
Bring me pine logs hither,
Thou and I will see him dine,
When we bear them thither.'
Page and monarch forth they went,
Forth they went together,
Through the cold wind's wild lament,
And the bitter weather.

'Sire, the night is darker now,
And the wind blows stronger,
Fails my heart, I know not how,
I can go no longer.'
'Mark my footsteps, my good page,
Tread thou in them boldly,
Thou shalt find the winter's rage,
Freeze thy blood less coldly.'

In his master's steps he trod,
Where the snow lay dinted,
Heat was in the very sod,
Which the Saint had printed.
Therefore, Christian men, be sure,
Wealth or rank possessing,
Ye who now will bless the poor,
Shall yourselves find blessing.

# HOLLY AND THE IVY

*Traditional English carol*

The holly and the ivy,
  When they are both full grown,
Of all the trees that are in the wood,
The holly bears the crown.

**Chorus:**

  O, the rising of the sun,
  And the running of the deer,
  The playing of the merry organ,
  Sweet singing in the choir.

The holly bears a blossom,
As white as lily flower,
And Mary bore sweet Jesus Christ,
To be our sweet Saviour.

**Chorus**

The holly bears a berry,
As red as any blood,
And Mary bore sweet Jesus Christ,
To do poor sinners good.

**Chorus**

The holly bears a prickle,
As sharp as any thorn,
And Mary bore sweet Jesus Christ,
On Christmas Day in the morn.

**Chorus**

The holly bears a bark,
As bitter as any gall,
And Mary bore sweet Jesus Christ,
For to redeem us all.

**Chorus**

# O Holy Night!

*Words by John Sullivan Dwight*

O holy night, the stars are brightly shining,
It is the night of the dear Saviour's birth.
Long lay the world in sin and error pining,
Till He appeared and the soul felt its worth.
A thrill of hope, the weary world rejoices,
For yonder breaks a new and glorious morn.

Fall on your knees! O hear the angel voices!
O night divine, O night when Christ was born;
O night, O holy night, O night divine!

Led by the light of faith serenely beaming,
With glowing hearts by His cradle we stand.
So led by light of a star sweetly gleaming,
Here come the Wise Men from Orient land.
The King of kings lay thus in lowly manger;
In all our trials born to be our friend.

He knows our need, to our weakness is no stranger,
Behold your King! Before him lowly bend!
Behold your King! Before him lowly bend!

Truly He taught us to love one another,
His law is love and His gospel is peace.
Chains shall He break, for the slave is our brother,
And in His name all oppression shall cease.
Sweet hymns of joy in grateful chorus raise we,
Let all within us praise His holy name.

Christ is the Lord! O praise His name forever,
His power and glory evermore proclaim!
His power and glory evermore proclaim!

# GOD REST YOU MERRY, GENTLEMEN

*Traditional carol*

God rest you merry, gentlemen,
Let nothing you dismay,
For Jesus Christ our Saviour
Was born upon this day,
To save us all from Satan's power
When we were gone astray.

**Chorus:**

O tidings of comfort and joy,
Comfort and joy,
O tidings of comfort and joy.

In Bethlehem, in Israel,
This blessèd Babe was born,
And laid within a manger
Upon this blessèd morn,
The which His Mother Mary
Did nothing take in scorn.

**Chorus**

From God our heavenly Father
A blessèd angel came,
And unto certain shepherds
Brought tidings of the same,
How that in Bethlehem was born
The Son of God by name.

**Chorus**

The shepherds at those tidings
Rejoicèd much in mind,
And left their flocks a-feeding
In tempest, storm and wind,
And went to Bethlehem straightway,
This blessèd Babe to find.

**Chorus**

But when to Bethlehem they came,
Whereat this Infant lay,
They found Him in a manger,
Where oxen feed on hay;
His mother Mary kneeling,
Unto the Lord did pray.

**Chorus**

Now to the Lord sing praises,
All you within this place,
And with true love and brotherhood
Each other now embrace;
This holy tide of Christmas
Doth bring redeeming grace.

**Chorus**

# O Little Town of Bethlehem

*Words by Phillips Brooks*

O little town of Bethlehem,
How still we see thee lie!
Above thy deep and dreamless sleep
The silent stars go by.
Yet in thy dark streets shineth
The everlasting light;
The hopes and fears of all the years
Are met in thee tonight.

O morning stars, together
Proclaim the holy birth!
And praises sing to God the King,
And peace to men on earth.
For Christ is born of Mary
And gathered all above,
While mortals sleep the angels keep
Their watch of wondering love.

How silently, how silently,
The wondrous gift is given!
So God imparts to human hearts
The blessings of His Heaven.
No ear may hear His coming;
But in this world of sin,
Where meek souls will receive Him still
The dear Christ enters in.

Where children pure and happy
Pray to the blessed Child,
Where Misery cries out to Thee,
Son of the Mother mild;
Where Charity stands watching,
And Faith holds wide the door,
The dark night wakes, the glory breaks,
And Christmas comes once more.

O holy Child of Bethlehem!
Descend to us we pray!
Cast out our sin and enter in,
Be born in us today.
We hear the Christmas angels
The great glad tidings tell;
O, come to us, abide with us,
Our Lord Emmanuel!

# HERE WE COME A-CAROLLING

*Traditional English carol*

Here we come a-carolling,
Among the leaves so green,
Here we come a-wand'ring,
So fair to be seen.

**Chorus:**

Love and joy come to you,
And to you glad Christmas too,
And God bless you and send you,
A Happy New Year,
And God send you a Happy New Year.

We are not daily beggars,
That beg from door to door,
But we are neighbours' children,
Whom you have seen before.

**Chorus**

Bring us out a table,
And spread it with a cloth.
Bring us out a mouldy cheese,
And some of your Christmas loaf.

**Chorus**

God bless the master of this house,
Likewise the mistress too,
And all the little children,
That round the table go.

**Chorus**

Good master and good mistress,
While you're sitting by the fire,
Pray think of us poor children,
Who are wandering in the mire.

**Chorus**

# THE FRIENDLY BEASTS

*Traditional English carol*

Jesus our brother, kind and good
Was humbly born in a stable rude
And the friendly beasts around Him stood,
Jesus our brother, kind and good.

'I,' said the donkey, shaggy and brown,
'I carried His mother up hill and down;
I carried her safely to Bethlehem town.'
'I,' said the donkey, shaggy and brown.

'I,' said the cow all white and red,
'I gave Him my manger for His bed;
I gave Him my hay to pillow His head.'
'I,' said the cow all white and red.

'I,' said the sheep with curly horn,
'I gave Him my wool for His blanket warm;
He wore my coat on Christmas morn.'
'I,' said the sheep with curly horn.

'I,' said the dove from the rafters high,
'I cooed Him to sleep so He would not cry;
We cooed Him to sleep, my mate and I.'
'I,' said the dove from the rafters high.

Thus every beast by some good spell,
In the stable dark was glad to tell
Of the gift he gave Emmanuel,
The gift he gave Emmanuel.

'I,' was glad to tell
Of the gift he gave Emmanuel,
The gift he gave Emmanuel.
Jesus our brother, kind and good.

# WHILE SHEPHERDS WATCHED THEIR FLOCKS BY NIGHT

*Words by Nahum Tate and Nicholas Brody*

While shepherds watched
their flocks by night,
All seated on the ground,
The angel of the Lord came down,
And glory shone around.

'Fear not,' he said, for mighty dread
Had seized their troubled minds.
'Glad tidings of great joy I bring
To you and all mankind.

'To you in David's town, this day
Is born of David's line
The Saviour who is Christ the Lord,
And this shall be the sign.

'The heavenly Babe you there shall find
To human view displayed,
All meanly wrapped in swaddling bands,
And in a manger laid.'

Thus spake the seraph, and forthwith
Appeared a shining throng
Of angels praising God, who thus
Addressed their joyful song.

'All glory be to God on high,
And to the earth be peace;
Goodwill henceforth from heaven to men
Begin and never cease!'

# I Saw Three Ships

*Traditional English carol*

I saw three ships come sailing in,
On Christmas Day, on Christmas Day;
I saw three ships come sailing in,
On Christmas Day in the morning.

And what was in those ships all three,
On Christmas Day, on Christmas Day;
And what was in those ships all three,
On Christmas Day in the morning?

The Virgin Mary and Christ were there,
On Christmas Day, on Christmas Day;
The Virgin Mary and Christ were there,
On Christmas Day in the morning.

Pray, whither sailed those ships all three,
On Christmas Day, on Christmas Day;
Pray, whither sailed those ships all three,
On Christmas Day in the morning?

O they sailed into Bethlehem,
On Christmas Day, on Christmas Day;
O they sailed into Bethlehem,
On Christmas Day in the morning.

And all the bells on earth shall ring,
On Christmas Day, on Christmas Day;
And all the bells on earth shall ring,
On Christmas Day in the morning.

And all the angels in heaven shall sing,
On Christmas Day, on Christmas Day;
And all the angels in heaven shall sing,
On Christmas Day in the morning.

And all the souls on earth shall sing,
On Christmas Day, on Christmas Day;
And all the souls on earth shall sing,
On Christmas Day in the morning.

Then let us all rejoice again,
On Christmas Day, on Christmas Day;
Then let us all rejoice again,
On Christmas Day in the morning.

# THE VIRGIN MARY HAD A BABY BOY

*Traditional West Indian carol*

The Virgin Mary had a baby boy,
The Virgin Mary had a baby boy,
The Virgin Mary had a baby boy,
And they say that His name was Jesus.

**Chorus:**

He come from the glory,
He come from the glorious kingdom.
He come from the glory,
He come from the glorious kingdom.
Oh yes, believer! Oh yes, believer!
He come from the glory,
He come from the glorious kingdom.

The angels sang when the baby born,
The angels sang when the baby born,
The angels sang when the baby born,
And proclaimed Him the Saviour Jesus.

**Chorus**

The shepherds came where the baby born,
The shepherds came where the baby born,
The shepherds came where the baby born,
And they say that His name was Jesus.

**Chorus**

The Wise Men saw where the baby born,
The Wise Men saw where the baby born,
The Wise Men saw where the baby born,
And they say that His name was Jesus.

**Chorus**

# THE FIRST NOEL

*Traditional carol*

The first Noel the angels did say,
Was to certain poor shepherds in fields as they lay;
In fields where they lay keeping their sheep,
On a cold winter's night that was so deep.

**Chorus:**

Noel, Noel, Noel, Noel,
Born is the King of Israel.

They looked up and saw a star,
Shining in the east, beyond them far;
And to the earth it gave great light,
And so it continued both day and night.

**Chorus**

And by the light of that same star,
Three Wise Men came from country far;
To seek for a King was their intent,
And to follow the star wherever it went.

**Chorus**

This star drew nigh to the north-west,
O'er Bethlehem it took its rest;
And there it did both stop and stay,
Right over the place where Jesus lay.

**Chorus**

Then entered in those Wise Men three,
Fell reverently upon their knee;
And offered there in his presence,
Their gold and myrrh and frankincense.

**Chorus**

Then let us all with one accord,
Sing praises to our heavenly Lord;
That hath made heaven and earth of naught,
And with his blood mankind hath bought.

**Chorus**

# WHAT CHILD IS THIS?

*Words by William Chatterton Dix*

What child is this, who, laid to rest,
On Mary's lap is sleeping,
Whom angels greet with anthems sweet,
While shepherds watch are keeping?
This, this is Christ the King,
Whom shepherds guard and angels sing;
Haste, haste to bring Him praise,
The Babe, the Son of Mary!

Why lies He in such mean estate,
Where ox and ass are feeding?
Come, have no fear; God's son is here.
His love all loves exceeding.
Nails, spear shall pierce Him through,
The Cross He bore for me, for you;
Hail, hail, the Saviour comes,
The Babe, the Son of Mary!

So bring Him incense, gold and myrrh;
Come, peasant, king, to own Him!
The King of kings salvation brings;
Let loving hearts enthrone Him!
Raise, raise the song on high!
While Mary sings a lullaby.
Joy, joy, for Christ is born,
The Babe, the Son of Mary!

# SILENT NIGHT

*Words by Joseph Mohr*

Silent night, holy night,
All is calm, all is bright;
Round yon virgin mother and Child.
Holy Infant, so tender and mild,
Sleep in heavenly peace,
Sleep in heavenly peace.

Silent night, holy night,
Shepherds quake at the sight;
Glories stream from heaven afar,
Heavenly hosts sing Alleluia!
Christ, the Saviour is born,
Christ, the Saviour is born!

Silent night, holy night,
Son of God, love's pure light;
Radiant beams from Thy holy face
With the dawn of redeeming grace,
Jesus, Lord, at Thy birth,
Jesus, Lord, at Thy birth.

**Repeat first verse**

# INFANT HOLY, INFANT LOWLY

*Traditional Polish carol*

Infant holy, infant lowly, for His bed a cattle stall;
Oxen lowing, little knowing, Christ the Babe is Lord of all.
Swift are winging, angels singing, noels ringing, tidings bringing,
Christ the Babe is Lord of all.
Christ the Babe is Lord of all.

Flocks were sleeping, shepherds keeping vigil till the morning new,
Saw the glory, heard the story, tidings of a Gospel true.
Thus rejoicing, free from sorrow, praises voicing, greet the morrow,
Christ the Babe was born for you.
Christ the Babe was born for you.

# Away in a Manger

*Traditional carol*

Away in a manger,
No crib for a bed,
The little Lord Jesus,
Laid down His sweet head.

The stars in the bright sky,
Looked down where He lay,
The little Lord Jesus,
Asleep on the hay.

The cattle are lowing,
The Baby awakes,
But little Lord Jesus,
No crying He makes.

I love Thee, Lord Jesus,
Look down from the sky,
And stay by my cradle,
'Til morning is nigh.

Be near me, Lord Jesus,
I ask Thee to stay,
Close by me forever,
And love me I pray.

Bless all the dear children,
In Thy tender care,
And take us to heaven,
To live with Thee there.

# WE WISH YOU A MERRY CHRISTMAS

*Traditional carol*

We wish you a merry Christmas,
We wish you a merry Christmas,
We wish you a merry Christmas,
And a happy New Year!

**Chorus:**
Good tidings we bring to you
and your kin;
We wish you a merry Christmas
and a happy New Year.

Oh bring us some figgy pudding,
Oh bring us some figgy pudding,
Oh bring us some figgy pudding,
And bring it right here.

**Chorus**

We won't go until we get some,
We won't go until we get some,
We won't go until we get some,
So bring it right here.

**Chorus**

We all like our figgy pudding,
We all like our figgy pudding,
We all like our figgy pudding,
With all its good cheer.

**Chorus**

***Repeat first verse***

# Christmas

# Stories

# A Christmas Carol

*Adapted from the story written by Charles Dickens*

Marley was dead. There is no doubt about that. Scrooge and he were partners for many years. But Scrooge never painted out Old Marley's name. There it stood, years afterwards, above the warehouse door: Scrooge and Marley.

Hard and sharp as flint, the cold within Scrooge froze his old features, nipped his pointed nose, shrivelled his cheeks, made his eyes red and his thin lips blue. He carried his own low temperature about with him, and didn't thaw it one degree at Christmas.

One Christmas Eve, old Ebenezer Scrooge sat busy in his counting house. The door was open, so that Scrooge could keep his eye on his clerk, Bob Cratchit, who was copying letters.

'A merry Christmas, uncle!' cried a cheerful voice. It was Scrooge's nephew, Fred.

'Bah!' said Scrooge. 'Humbug!'

'Christmas a humbug, uncle!' said Fred. 'You don't mean that, I am sure?'

'I do,' said Scrooge. 'Merry Christmas! What right have you to be merry? You're poor enough.'

'What right have you to be dismal?' returned Fred gaily, 'You're rich enough.'

Scrooge said, 'Bah!' again, and followed it up with 'Humbug!'

'Don't be angry, uncle. Come! Dine with us tomorrow.'

Scrooge refused and his nephew left.

At the end of the day, Bob Cratchit snuffed his candle out and put on his hat.

'You'll want all day off tomorrow, I suppose?' said Scrooge.

'If it's convenient, sir,' said Bob.

'I suppose you must have the whole day. But be here all the earlier next morning.'

The clerk promised that he would, and Scrooge walked out with a growl.

Scrooge went home. The yard was dark as he put his key in the lock. Strangely, he saw the face of his dead partner, Marley, in the door knocker. Then all of a sudden the face was gone.

He paused for a moment before he shut the door, and looked cautiously behind it, but seeing nothing unusual, he closed it with a bang.

'Humbug!' said Scrooge as he walked through the house and prepared for bed. He sat down and his glance happened to rest upon a bell that hung in the room. As he looked, he saw the bell begin to swing. Soon it rang out loudly, and so did every bell in the house.

All of a sudden, the bells ceased, and there was a clanking noise, as if someone were dragging a heavy chain in the cellar. The cellar door flew open with a booming sound, and Scrooge heard the noise coming up the stairs, then straight towards his door.

'It's humbug still!' said Scrooge. 'I won't believe it.'

His colour changed, though, when a transparent figure came through the heavy door, and passed into the room before his eyes.

Scrooge, sharp and cold as ever, said, 'Who are you?'

'Ask me who I *was*.'

'Who *were* you, then?' said Scrooge, raising his voice.

'In life I was your partner, Jacob Marley. You don't believe in me,' observed the Ghost.

'I don't,' said Scrooge.

At this the spirit raised a frightful cry, and shook its chain with such an appalling noise, that Scrooge held on tight to his chair.

'You are chained,' said Scrooge, trembling. 'Tell me why?'

'I wear the chain I forged in life by being greedy and doing wrong to others,' replied the Ghost. 'I am here tonight to warn you that you have yet a chance and hope of escaping my fate, Ebenezer. You will be haunted by Three Spirits.'

'I – I think I'd rather not,' said Scrooge.

'Without their visits,' said the Ghost, 'you cannot hope to shun the path I tread. Expect the first when the bell tolls one.'

The spectre floated out into the bleak, dark night. Scrooge closed the window and examined the door by which the Ghost had entered. He tried to say 'Humbug!' but stopped at the first syllable. He went straight to bed without undressing, and fell asleep instantly.

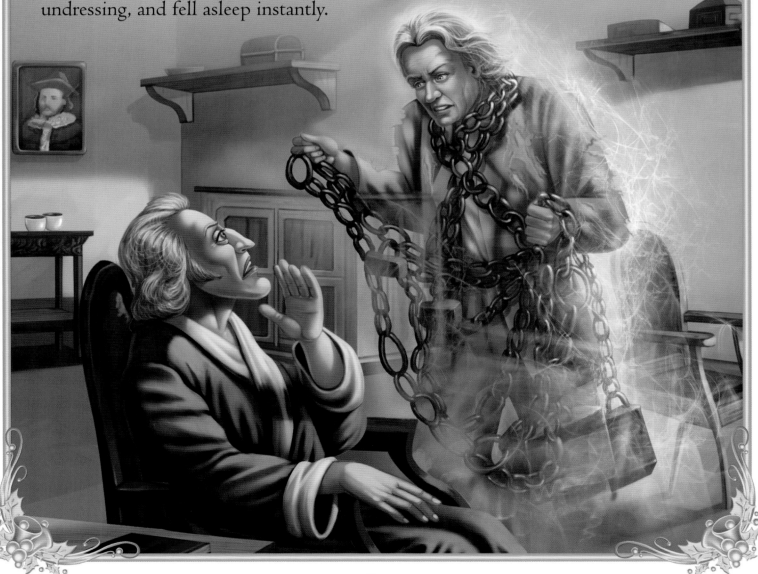

When Scrooge awoke it was dark. He listened for the hour. It chimed twelve! Scrooge remembered that Marley's Ghost had warned him of a visitation when the bell tolled one. He decided to lie awake until the hour passed.

When the hour bell sounded, the curtains of his bed were drawn aside by a hand. Scrooge saw a strange figure — like a child, yet also like an old man. It wore a tunic of the purest white. It held a branch of fresh green holly. From the crown of its head there sprung a bright clear jet of light.

'Are you the Spirit, sir, whose coming was foretold to me?' asked Scrooge.

'I am!'

The voice was soft and gentle.

'Who and what are you?' Scrooge demanded.

'I am the Ghost of Christmas Past.'

It put out its strong hand as it spoke, and clasped him gently by the arm.

'Rise and walk with me!'

He rose, and they passed through the wall and onto an open country road. The city had vanished.

'Good Heaven!' said Scrooge as he looked about. 'I was a boy here!'

As they walked along the road some boys went by. They were in great spirits and shouted to each other.

'These are but shadows of the things that have been,' said the Ghost. 'They cannot see us.'

As the travellers came, Scrooge knew every one. Why did his heart leap up as they went past? Why was he filled with gladness when he heard them say 'Merry Christmas'? What was merry Christmas to Scrooge?

'The school is not quite deserted,' said the Ghost. 'A solitary child, neglected by his friends, is left there still.'

Scrooge said he knew it and he sobbed.

They left the road and approached the school. In a bare, melancholy room sat a lonely boy reading at a desk. Scrooge sat down and wept, because the poor forgotten boy was himself as a child.

The Ghost waved its hand, saying as it did so, 'Let us see another Christmas!'

They left the school behind them and were now in a busy city. It was Christmas time again.

The Ghost stopped at a warehouse door, and asked Scrooge if he knew it.

'Know it!' said Scrooge. 'Was I apprenticed here?'

They went in. There was an old gentleman in a wig, sitting behind a high desk. Scrooge cried in great excitement, 'Why, it's old Fezziwig! Bless his heart, it's Fezziwig alive again!'

Old Fezziwig laid down his pen, and called out, in a jovial voice, 'Yo ho, there, Ebenezer!'

Scrooge's former self, now grown a young man, came briskly in.

'No more work tonight. Christmas Eve, Ebenezer!'

In came a fiddler and in came Mrs Fezziwig, smiling. In came all the young men and women employed in the business.

There were dances, and there was cake, and there were mince pies.

When the clock struck eleven, the ball broke up. Mr and Mrs Fezziwig stood on either side the door, shook hands with every person and wished them all a merry Christmas.

Scrooge's heart and soul were in the scene, and with his former self. He remembered everything, and enjoyed everything.

Scrooge felt the Spirit's glance, and stopped.

'What is the matter?' asked the Ghost.

'Nothing,' said Scrooge.

'Something, I think?' the Ghost insisted.

'I should like to be able to say a word or two to my clerk Bob Cratchit just now. That's all.'

'My time grows short,' observed the Spirit. 'Quick!'

Again Scrooge saw himself. He was older now. He was not alone, but sat by the side of a fair young girl in whose eyes there were tears.

'It matters little,' she said softly. 'Money is more important to you than I am. If it can cheer and comfort you in time to come, I have no cause to grieve. I can't marry you, Ebenezer.'

'Spirit!' said Scrooge in a broken voice, 'remove me from this place. I cannot bear it! Take me back! Haunt me no longer!'

Scrooge was exhausted and, overcome with drowsiness. He realised he was in his own bedroom. He barely had time to stagger to bed before he sank into a heavy sleep.

After waking, Scrooge waited for the second messenger. But, when no shape appeared, he was taken with a violent fit of trembling. At last, he got up softly, and shuffled in his slippers to the door.

The moment Scrooge's hand was on the lock, a strange voice called his name.

'Come in!' exclaimed the Ghost. 'Come in and know me better, man!'

Scrooge entered timidly, and hung his head before this Spirit.

'I am the Ghost of Christmas Present,' said the Spirit. 'Look upon me!'

Scrooge did so. It was clothed in one simple deep green robe, bordered with white fur. Its feet were bare and on its head it wore a holly wreath. Its dark brown curls were long and free. It had a friendly face, sparkling eyes and a cheery voice.

'Touch my robe!' said the Spirit.

Scrooge did as he was told, and held the robe tightly. The room vanished and they stood in the city streets on Christmas morning. The people were jovial and full of glee. The Spirit took Scrooge to Bob Cratchit's house.

Mrs Cratchit was preparing Christmas dinner. The older children helped while the younger Cratchits danced about the table. In came Bob with Tiny Tim upon his shoulder. Tiny Tim carried a little crutch, and had iron frames on his legs.

The Cratchits' Christmas dinner was a small one for a large family, but they were happy, grateful, pleased with one another and contented. After dinner Bob proposed a toast: 'A merry Christmas to us all, my dears. God bless us!' The family echoed his toast.

'God bless us every one!' said Tiny Tim, the last of all. He sat very close to his father's side. Bob held Tim's little hand in his.

'Spirit,' said Scrooge with an interest he had never felt before, 'tell me if Tiny Tim will live.'

'I see a vacant seat,' replied the Ghost, 'and a crutch without an owner.'

'No, no,' said Scrooge. 'Oh, no, kind Spirit! Say he will be spared.'

Scrooge was overcome grief.

As the family faded, Scrooge kept his eye upon them, and especially on Tiny Tim, until the last.

It was a great surprise to Scrooge to hear a hearty laugh and to suddenly find himself in a bright, gleaming room, with the Spirit standing smiling by his side.

'Ha, ha!' laughed Scrooge's nephew, Fred. 'Ha, ha, ha!' Fred's wife and their guests laughed too.

'He said that Christmas was a humbug, as I live!' cried Fred. 'He believed it, too! He's a comical old fellow and not so pleasant as he might be, but I have nothing to say against him.'

'I have no patience with him,' said Fred's wife.

'Oh, I have!' said Scrooge's nephew. 'I am sorry for him; I couldn't be angry with him if I tried. Who suffers by his ill whims? Himself always. A merry Christmas and a happy New Year to the old man, whatever he is!'

Scrooge felt so lighthearted that he would have thanked Fred if the Ghost had given him time. But the whole scene disappeared.

Scrooge looked for the Ghost, but it was gone. Instead, he saw a new Phantom, draped and hooded, coming like a mist along the ground towards him. The Phantom was shrouded in a deep black garment, which left nothing of it visible, except one outstretched hand. The Spirit did not speak.

'I am in the presence of the Ghost of Christmas Yet to Come?' said Scrooge.

The Spirit did not answer, but pointed onward with its hand.

'You are about to show me shadows of the things that have not happened?'

The Spirit seemed to nod its head slightly.

'Ghost of the Future!' exclaimed Scrooge, 'I fear you more than any spectre I have seen. But, as I hope to live to be a different man than I was, I am prepared to bear you company. Will you not speak to me?'

It gave him no reply. The hand was pointed straight before them.

'Lead on, Spirit!' said Scrooge.

The phantom moved away and Scrooge followed.

The Spirit stopped beside a little knot of businessmen. Scrooge listened to them.

'I don't know much about it. I only know he's dead,' said one.

'What has he done with his money?' asked another.

'I haven't heard,' said the first man. 'He hasn't left it to *me*. That's all I know.'

This pleasantry was received with a general laugh.

The Phantom glided on. The scene changed, and Scrooge saw a bare, uncurtained bed, on which there lay the covered body of a man — all alone, with no one to weep for him.

The Spirit continued on and Scrooge joined it in a churchyard. The Spirit stood among the graves, and pointed to one.

Scrooge crept towards it, trembling as he went and, following the finger, read upon the stone of the neglected grave his own name, EBENEZER SCROOGE.

'Am *I* that man who lay upon the bed?' he cried.

The finger pointed from the grave to him, and back again.

'No, Spirit! Oh no, no!' said Scrooge, 'May I yet change these shadows you have shown me?'

The hand trembled.

'I will honour Christmas in my heart, and try to keep it all the year. Oh, tell me I may wipe away the writing on this stone!'

Holding up his hands in a last prayer to have his fate reversed, he saw the Phantom's hood and dress shrink and then collapse.

Scrooge was back in his own bed in his own room. Best and happiest of all, there was still time to make amends!

Scrooge was laughing and crying at once. 'I am as light as a feather, I am as happy as an angel, I am as merry as a schoolboy. A merry Christmas to everybody! A happy New Year to all the world!'

Running to the window, he opened it and put out his head. 'What's today?' cried Scrooge, calling down to a boy below.

'Today!' replied the boy. 'Why, CHRISTMAS DAY.'

'It's Christmas Day!' said Scrooge. 'I haven't missed it. Do you know the shop in the next street? Have they sold the prize turkey that was hanging up there? The big one?'

'What – the one as big as me?' returned the boy. 'It's hanging there now.'

'Is it?' said Scrooge. 'Go and buy it. Come back with it in less than five minutes, and I'll give you half a crown!'

The boy was off like a shot.

'I'll send it to Bob Cratchit's,' whispered Scrooge with a laugh. 'It's twice the size of Tiny Tim!' He wrote out the address with a shaking hand, paid for the turkey when it arrrived and sent it to Bob Cratchit's, chuckling all the while.

Scrooge dressed himself in his best and went out. He gave each person passing by a delighted smile.

He went to his nephew's house for dinner. Fred was so glad to see his uncle it is a mercy he didn't shake his arm off. Scrooge felt at home in five minutes and enjoyed a wonderful Christmas party!

Scrooge was early at the office next morning. Bob Cratchit was late. Scrooge sat with his door wide open.

'Hallo!' growled Scrooge in his usual voice. 'What do you mean by coming here at this time of day?'

'I am very sorry, sir,' said Bob.

'Step this way, sir, if you please,' said Scrooge.

'It's only once a year, sir,' pleaded Bob. 'It shall not be repeated.'

'Now, I'll tell you what, my friend,' said Scrooge. 'I am not going to stand this sort of thing any longer. And therefore,' he continued, 'I am about to raise your salary! A merry Christmas, Bob!' said Scrooge earnestly. 'A merrier Christmas, Bob, than I have given you for many a year! I'll raise your salary, and try to help your struggling family.'

Scrooge was better than his word. He did it all, and infinitely more; and to Tiny Tim, who did NOT die, he was a second father. He became as good a friend, as good a master and as good a man as the good old city knew.

It was always said of him afterwards that he knew how to keep Christmas well. May that be truly said of all of us! And so, as Tiny Tim observed, God bless us, every one!

# The Night Before Christmas

*Written by Clement Clarke Moore*

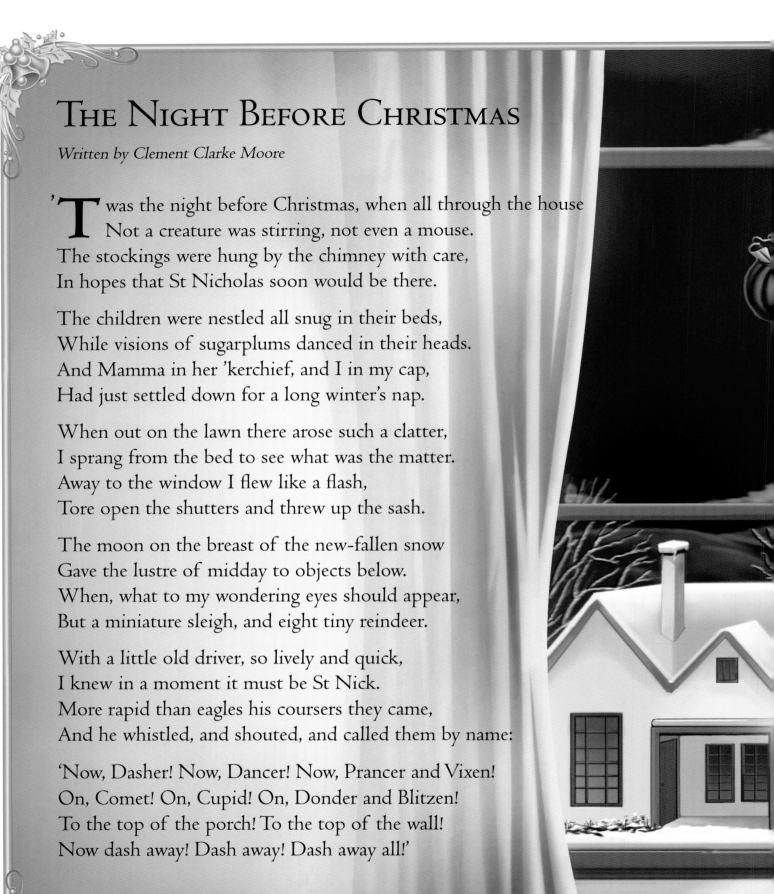

'Twas the night before Christmas, when all through the house
Not a creature was stirring, not even a mouse.
The stockings were hung by the chimney with care,
In hopes that St Nicholas soon would be there.

The children were nestled all snug in their beds,
While visions of sugarplums danced in their heads.
And Mamma in her 'kerchief, and I in my cap,
Had just settled down for a long winter's nap.

When out on the lawn there arose such a clatter,
I sprang from the bed to see what was the matter.
Away to the window I flew like a flash,
Tore open the shutters and threw up the sash.

The moon on the breast of the new-fallen snow
Gave the lustre of midday to objects below.
When, what to my wondering eyes should appear,
But a miniature sleigh, and eight tiny reindeer.

With a little old driver, so lively and quick,
I knew in a moment it must be St Nick.
More rapid than eagles his coursers they came,
And he whistled, and shouted, and called them by name:

'Now, Dasher! Now, Dancer! Now, Prancer and Vixen!
On, Comet! On, Cupid! On, Donder and Blitzen!
To the top of the porch! To the top of the wall!
Now dash away! Dash away! Dash away all!'

As dry leaves that before the wild hurricane fly,
When they meet with an obstacle, mount to the sky;
So up to the housetop the coursers they flew,
With the sleigh full of toys, and St Nicholas too.

And then, in a twinkling, I heard on the roof
The prancing and pawing of each little hoof.
As I drew in my head, and was turning around,
Down the chimney St Nicholas came with a bound.

He was dressed all in fur, from his head to his foot,
And his clothes were all tarnished with ashes and soot.
A bundle of toys he had flung on his back,
And he looked like a peddler, just opening his pack.

His eyes, how they twinkled! His dimples, how merry!
His cheeks were like roses, his nose like a cherry!
His droll little mouth was drawn up like a bow,
And the beard on his chin was as white as the snow.

The stump of a pipe he held tight in his teeth,
And the smoke it encircled his head like a wreath.
He had a broad face and a little round belly,
That shook when he laughed, like a bowl full of jelly.

He was chubby and plump, a right jolly old elf,
And I laughed when I saw him, in spite of myself.
A wink of his eye and a twist of his head,
Soon gave me to know I had nothing to dread.

He spoke not a word, but went straight to his work,
And filled all the stockings, then turned with a jerk.
And laying his finger aside of his nose,
And giving a nod, up the chimney he rose.

He sprang to his sleigh, to his team gave a whistle,
And away they all flew like the down of a thistle.
But I heard him exclaim, 'ere he drove out of sight,
'Happy Christmas to all, and to all a good night!'

# SANTA'S HELPERS

*Written by M. Nora Boylan*

The fairies and brownies on last Christmastide
Decided to open their hearts very wide,
And spend extra time, throughout the whole year,
In helping their grandfather – Santa Claus dear.

'Our fingers are nimble. We'll quickly make toys
Enough to supply all the girls and the boys,
And Santa may watch us to see if it's right,
So all will be ready before Christmas night.'

Then bravely they all went to work with a will,
And soon all was quiet in workshop and mill;
For old Santa said, 'Enough, and well done,
We've toys enough now to make all kinds of fun.'

We thank you, old Santa, and your helpers, too,
For all of the many kind things that you do;
And should you need more help in making your toys,
Just call on your small friends, the girls and the boys.

# LITTLE GIRL'S CHRISTMAS

*Adapted from the story written by Winnifred E. Lincoln*

It was Christmas Eve, and Little Girl had just hung up her stocking by the fireplace – all ready for Santa when he slipped down the chimney. She knew he was coming, because – well, because it was Christmas Eve, and because he always had come to leave gifts for her on all the other Christmas Eves that she could remember.

Still, she wasn't satisfied. Way down in her heart she was a little uncertain. You see, when you have never really and truly seen a person with your very own eyes, it's hard to feel as if you exactly believe in him.

'Oh, he'll come,' said Little Girl. 'I just know he will be here before morning, but somehow I wish ... '

'Well, what do you wish?' said a tiny voice close by her – so close that Little Girl fairly jumped when she heard it.

'Why, I wish I could *see* Santa myself. I'd just like to go and see his house and his workshop, and ride in his sleigh, and meet Mrs Claus. It would be such fun, and then I'd *know* for sure.'

'Why don't you go, then?' said the tiny voice. 'It's easy enough. Just try on these shoes, and take this light in your hand, and you'll find your way all right.'

So Little Girl looked down on the hearth, and there were two little shoes side by side, and a little spark of a light close to them. Little Girl could hardly wait to pull off her slippers and try the shoes on. They looked as if they were too small, but they weren't – they fitted exactly right! Just as Little Girl had put them both on and had taken the light in her hand, along came a little breath of wind, and away she went up the chimney, along with ever so many other little sparks, past the soot fairies, and out into the open air, where Jack Frost and the star beams were busy making the world look pretty for Christmas.

Away went Little Girl – two shoes, bright light and all – higher and higher, until she looked like a star up in the sky. It was the funniest thing, but she seemed to know the way perfectly. You see, it was a straight road all the way, and when one doesn't have to think about turning to the right or the left, it makes things much easier. Pretty soon Little Girl noticed that there was a bright light all around her, and right away something down in her heart began to make her feel very happy indeed. She didn't know that the Christmas spirits and little Christmas fairies were all around her and even right inside her, because she couldn't see a single one of them.

Little Girl felt as if she wanted to laugh and sing and be glad. It made her remember the sick boy who lived next door, and she said to herself that she would take one of her prettiest picture books to him in the morning, so that he could have something to make him happy all day. By and by, when the bright light all around her had grown much brighter, Little Girl saw a path right in front of her, all straight and trim, leading up a hill to a big house with ever so many windows. When she had gone just a bit nearer, she saw candles in every window, red and green and yellow ones, and every one burning brightly, so Little Girl knew right away that these were Christmas candles to light her on her journey. Something told her that this was Santa's house, and that pretty soon she would perhaps see Santa himself.

Just as she neared the steps and before she could possibly have had time to ring the bell, the door opened itself as wide as could be. There stood – not Santa himself – but a funny little man with slender little legs and a roly-poly stomach, which shook every now and then when he laughed. You would have known right away, just as Little Girl knew, that he was a very happy little man, and you would have guessed right away, too, that the reason he was so roly-poly was because he laughed and chuckled and smiled all the time. Quick as a wink, he pulled off his little peaked red cap, smiled the broadest kind of a smile, and said, 'Merry Christmas! Merry Christmas! Come in! Come in!'

So in went Little Girl, holding fast to the little man's hand, and when she was really inside there was the jolliest, reddest fire all glowing and snapping, and there were the little man's brothers and sisters. They said their names were 'Merry Christmas', and 'Good Cheer', and ever so many other jolly-sounding things. There were so many of them that Little Girl just knew she never could count them, no matter how long she tried.

All around her were bundles and boxes and piles of toys and games, and Little Girl knew that these were all ready and waiting to be loaded into Santa's big sleigh. His reindeer would whirl them away over cloud-tops and snowdrifts to the little people down below who had left their stockings all ready for him. Pretty soon all the little Good Cheer brothers began to hurry and bustle and carry out the bundles as fast as they could to the steps where Little Girl could hear jingling bells and stamping hoofs. So Little Girl picked up some bundles and skipped along too, for she wanted to help a bit herself. There in the yard stood the *biggest* sleigh that Little Girl had ever seen. The reindeer were all stamping and prancing and jingling the bells on their harnesses, because they were so eager to be on their way around the earth once more.

She could hardly wait for Santa to come. Just as she had begun to wonder where he was, the door opened again and out came a whole forest of Christmas trees. At least, it looked just as if a whole forest had started out for a walk somewhere, but a second glance showed Little Girl that there were thousands of Christmas sprites, and that each one carried a tree or a big Christmas wreath on his back. Behind them all, she could hear someone laughing loudly, and talking in a big, jovial voice that sounded as if he were good friends with the whole world.

Straightaway she knew that Santa himself was coming. Little Girl's heart went pit-a-pat for a minute while she wondered if Santa would notice her. She didn't have to wonder long, for he spied her at once and said, 'Bless my soul! Who's this? And where did you come from?'

Little Girl thought perhaps she might be afraid to answer him, but she wasn't one bit afraid. You see he had such a kind little twinkle in his eyes that she felt happy right away as she replied, 'Oh, I'm Little Girl, and I wanted so much to see Santa that I just came, and here I am!'

'Ho, ho, ho, ho, ho!' laughed Santa, 'And here you are! Wanted to see Santa, did you, and so you came! Now that's very nice, and it's too bad I'm in such a hurry, for I should like nothing better than to show you about and give you a really good time. But you see it is quarter to twelve now, and I must be on my way at once, or else I'll never reach that first chimney-top by midnight. I'd call Mrs Claus and ask her to make you some supper, but she is busy finishing dolls' clothes, which must be done before morning. Is there anything that you would like, Little Girl?'

Santa put his big warm hand on Little Girl's head and she felt its warmth and kindness down to her very heart. You see, my dears, that even though Santa was in such a great hurry, he wasn't too busy to stop and make someone happy for a minute, even if it was someone no bigger than Little Girl.

So she smiled back into Santa's face and said, 'Oh, Santa, if I could only ride down with you behind those splendid reindeer! I'd love to go; won't you *please* take me? I'm so small that I won't take up much room on the seat, and I'll keep very still and not bother you one bit!'

Then Santa laughed *such* a laugh — big and loud and rollicking. He said, 'Wants a ride, does she? Well, well, shall we take her, little elves? Shall we take her, little fairies? Shall we take her, good reindeer?'

And all the little elves hopped and skipped and brought Little Girl a sprig of holly; and all the little fairies bowed and smiled and brought her a bit of mistletoe; and all the good reindeer jingled their bells loudly, which meant, 'Oh, yes! Let's take her!' And before Little Girl could even think, she found herself all tucked up in the big fur robes beside Santa. Away they went, right out into the air, over the clouds and on toward earth, whose lights Little Girl began to see twinkling away down below her. She knew that Santa would slip down a chimney in a minute. How she wanted to go, too!

So, just as Little Girl was wishing as hard as she could wish, she heard a tiny voice say, 'Hold tight to his arm! Hold tight to his arm!' So she held Santa's arm tight and close. Santa shouldered his pack and with a bound and a slide, they were right in the middle of a room where there was a fireplace and stockings.

Just then Santa noticed Little Girl. He had forgotten all about her for a minute, and he was very much surprised to find that she had come, too.

'Bless my soul!' Santa said. 'Where did you come from, Little Girl? And how in the world can we both get back up that chimney again? It's easy enough to slide down, but it's quite another matter to climb up again!' Santa looked worried.

But Little Girl was beginning to feel very tired by this time, for she had had a very exciting evening, so she said, 'Oh, never mind me, Santa. I've had such a good time, and I'd just as soon stay here a while as not. I believe I'll curl up on this hearth-rug a few minutes and have a little nap, for it looks as warm and cosy as our own hearth-rug at home, and – why, it is our own hearth and it's my own nursery, for there is Teddy Bear in his chair where I leave him every night.'

And Little Girl turned to thank Santa and say goodbye to him, but either he had gone very quickly, or else she had fallen asleep very quickly – she never could tell which – for the next thing she knew, Daddy was holding her in his arms and was saying, 'What is my Little Girl doing here? She must go to bed, for it's Christmas Eve, and old Santa won't come if he thinks there are any little folks about.'

But Little Girl knew better than that, and when she began to tell him all about it, and how the Christmas fairies had welcomed her, and how Santa had given her such a fine ride, Daddy laughed and said, 'You've been dreaming, my dear.'

But Little Girl knew better than that, too, for tight in her hand she held some holly berries which one of the Christmas elves had placed there. More than that, she had fallen asleep on the hearth-rug, just where Santa had left her, and that was the best proof of all.

# THE GIFT OF THE MAGI

*Adapted from the story written by O. Henry*

One dollar and eighty-seven cents. That was all. Three times Della counted it. One dollar and eighty-seven cents. And the next day would be Christmas. There was clearly nothing to do but flop down on the shabby little couch and howl. So Della did it.

When Della finished her cry she powdered her cheeks. She stood by the window and looked out at a grey cat walking along a grey fence in a grey backyard. Tomorrow would be Christmas Day, and she had only $1.87 with which to buy her husband Jim a present. She had been saving every penny she could for months, with this result. Only $1.87 to buy a present for Jim. Her Jim. Many a happy hour she had spent planning for something nice for him. Something fine and rare.

There was a large, high mirror between the windows of the room. Suddenly Della whirled from the window and stood before the mirror. Her eyes were shining brilliantly, but her face had lost its colour. Rapidly she pulled down her hair and let it fall to its full length.

Now, there were two possessions in which Della and Jim both took a mighty pride. One was Jim's gold watch that had been his father's and his grandfather's. The other was Della's hair. Della's beautiful hair fell about her, rippling and shining like a cascade of brown waters. It reached below her knees and made itself almost a garment for her. And then she did it up again, nervously and quickly.

On went her old brown jacket; on went her old brown hat. With a whirl of her skirts and with the brilliant sparkle still in her eyes, she fluttered out the door and down the stairs to the street.

She stopped at a shop with a sign that read: 'Madame Sofronie, Hair Goods of All Kinds.' One flight up Della ran, then collected herself, panting.

'Will you buy my hair?' asked Della.

'I buy hair,' said Madame. 'Take yer hat off and let's have a look at it.'

Della let down her hair.

'Twenty dollars,' said Madame, lifting Della's hair and examining it closely.

'Give it to me quick,' said Della.

The next two hours tripped by on rosy wings. Della searched the stores for Jim's present.

She found it at last. It surely had been made for Jim and no one else. There was no other like it in any of the stores, and she had turned all of them inside out. It was a platinum fob chain, simple in design, declaring its value by substance alone and not by being showy. It was even worthy of The Watch. As soon as she saw it she knew that it must be Jim's. It was like him. Quiet and valuable – the description applied to both. Twenty-one dollars they took from her for it, and she hurried home with the eighty-seven cents. With that chain on his watch Jim might be properly anxious about the time in any company. Grand as the watch was, he sometimes looked at it on the sly on account of the old leather strap he used in place of a chain.

When Della reached home, she got out her curling irons and lighted the gas and went to work repairing her hair. Within forty minutes her head was covered with tiny close-lying curls that made her look wonderfully like a truant schoolboy. She looked at her reflection in the mirror long, carefully and critically.

'If Jim doesn't kill me,' she said to herself, 'before he takes a second look at me, he'll say I look like a Coney Island chorus girl. But what could I do? Oh, what could I do with a dollar and eighty-seven cents?'

At seven o'clock the coffee was made and the frying pan was hot on the back of the stove.

Jim was never late. Della doubled the fob chain in her hand and sat on the corner of the table near the door that he always entered. Then she heard his step on the stair down on the first flight, and she turned white for just a moment. She had a habit of saying little silent prayers about the simplest everyday things, and now she whispered, 'Please, God, make him think I am still pretty.'

The door opened and Jim stepped in and closed it. He looked thin and very serious. He needed a new overcoat and he was without gloves.

Jim stopped inside the door. His eyes were fixed upon Della. There was an expression in them that she could not read, and it terrified her. It was not anger, nor surprise, nor disapproval, nor horror, nor any of the sentiments that she had been prepared for. He simply stared at her fixedly with that peculiar expression on his face.

'Jim, darling,' Della cried, 'don't look at me that way. I had my hair cut off and sold it because I couldn't live through Christmas without giving you a present. It'll grow out again. My hair grows awfully fast. Say "Merry Christmas" Jim, and let's be happy. You don't know what a beautiful gift I've got for you.'

'You've cut off your hair?' asked Jim in confusion.

'Cut it off and sold it,' said Della. 'Don't you like me just as well, anyhow? I'm me without my hair, ain't I?'

Jim looked about the room curiously.

'You say your hair is gone?' he asked again.

'You needn't look for it,' said Della. 'It's sold, I tell you. It's Christmas Eve. Maybe the hairs of my head were numbered,' she went on with a sudden serious sweetness, 'but nobody could ever count my love for you.'

Out of his trance Jim seemed quickly to wake. He embraced his Della.

Then Jim drew a package from his overcoat pocket.

'Don't make any mistake, Dell,' he said. 'A haircut couldn't make me like my girl any less. But if you'll unwrap that package, you may see why you had me going a while at first.'

Her fingers nimbly tore at the string and paper. There was an ecstatic scream of joy, which quickly changed to hysterical tears and wails.

For there lay The Combs — the set of combs that Della had worshipped for so long in a Broadway window. Beautiful combs — pure tortoiseshell with jewelled rims. They were expensive combs, and her heart had simply yearned for them without the least hope of owning them. And now they were hers, but the tresses they should have adorned were gone.

But she hugged them, and at length she was able to look up with a smile and say, 'My hair grows so fast, Jim!'

And then Della leaped up and cried, 'Oh, Oh!'

Jim had not yet seen his beautiful present.

Della held out the chain to him eagerly upon her open palm. The precious metal seemed to flash with a reflection of her bright spirit.

'Isn't it a dandy, Jim? I hunted all over town to find it. You'll have to look at the time a hundred times a day now. Give me your watch. I want to see how it looks on it.'

Instead of obeying, Jim tumbled down on the couch and put his hand under the back of his head and smiled.

'Dell,' said he, 'let's put our Christmas presents away and keep 'em a while. They're too nice to use just now. I sold the watch to get the money to buy your combs!'

*The magi were wise men — wonderfully wise men — who brought gifts to the Babe in the manger. They invented the art of giving Christmas presents. Being wise, their gifts were no doubt wise ones. And here I have related to you the uneventful tale of two foolish people who most unwisely sacrificed for each other the greatest treasures of their home. But in a last word, let it be said that of all who give gifts these two were the wisest. And all who give and receive gifts are the wisest. They are the magi.*